A Book

There is no frigate like a book
To take us lands away,
Nor any coursers like a page
Of prancing poetry.
This traverse may the poorest take
Without oppress of toll;
How frugal is the chariot
That bears a human soul!

Emily Dickinson

The Paintbox

'Cobalt and umber and ultramarine,
Ivory black and emerald green —
What shall I paint to give pleasure to you?'
'Paint for me somebody utterly new.'

'I have painted you tigers in crimson and white.'
'The colours were good and you painted a-right.'
'I have painted the cook and a camel in blue
And a panther in purple.' 'You painted them true.

Now mix me a colour that nobody knows
And paint me a country where nobody goes
And put in it people a little like you,
Watching a unicorn drinking the dew.'

E. V. Rieu

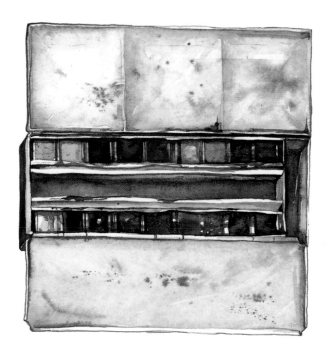

For Ffion and her dog, more lap dog than lone dog — J. M.

I would like to thank the friends who helped to form and shape this book. Tessa for the long nights poring over poetry books, all those who suggested favourite poems for inclusion, my children and Robin for their support, and I would like to dedicate 'Fern Hill' to Colin Leyshon, who liked nothing more than to roll the words of poets around and had an enviable memory for poetry and song.

Barefoot Books
124 Walcot Street
Bath BA1 5BG

This book has been printed on 100% acid-free paper

Graphic design by Sarah Hodder, London
Colour separation by Bright Arts, Singapore
Printed and bound in China by Printplus Ltd
This book was typeset in Centaur/Centaur Italic
The illustrations were prepared in Winsor and Newton Artists' watercolour on Arches hot-pressed paper

Hardback ISBN 1-905236-55-7

British Cataloguing-in-Publication Data:
a catalogue record for this book is available from the British Library

7 9 8 6

The Barefoot Book of
CLASSIC
POEMS

Best wishes
Jackie Morris

Compiled and illustrated by Jackie Morris

Introduced by Carol Ann Duffy

Barefoot Books
Celebrating Art and Story

Introduction

Here is the gorgeous *Barefoot Book of Classic Poems*, compiled and beautifully illustrated by Jackie Morris. The poems here are 'classic' because, although their authors are no longer living, they continue to shine brightly in the English language — true stars. As E. V. Rieu's opening poem may suggest, these are poems that persist in managing to be new. This is an anthology for adults to re-discover, for children to newly delight in, and for both to share together. It provides a place, both magical and familiar, for our imaginations to live in.

Some of the poems here are among the most enduring children's poetry we have. They are almost part of our DNA — 'The Owl and the Pussy-Cat', 'The Jabberwocky', 'The Tyger', 'maggie and milly and molly and may'. The rich illustrations to these familiar classics sing on the page, too. Shakespeare, whose language remains the true expression of our psyche, is here; along with Milton, Donne, Byron and Wordsworth. Their poems read as vividly now as in the gone days when they were written. Sylvia Plath, Stevie Smith and Kathleen Raine are as powerfully present as Elizabeth Barrett Browning, timelessly counting the ways in which she loves. There are poems from the unique geniuses of Walt Whitman

and Dylan Thomas, whose glorious 'Fern Hill' is the soul of childhood; from the War poets Isaac Rosenberg and Siegfried Sassoon; and from those formal masters, Byron and Auden. Throughout the book, there are real treasures to be found. There are surprising juxtapositions and deep echoes. As with all the best anthologies, the individual poems call and respond to each other across the pages and the ages.

Reading Jackie Morris's selection, what struck me forcibly was the truly *human* quality of the contents. From birth, when, as Sylvia Plath says, love sets us going like a fat gold watch, through childhood, to our relationship with the natural world, our journeys, love, war, belief and death, the poems open up real and imaginary ways of seeing, remembering or wondering. Poetry, of all the arts, offers us moments in language which preserve or celebrate, explore or elegise, transform or enhance our human joys and sadnesses. The best of poetry is memorable, as prayers are, and in this wonderful selection of classic poems both young and older readers will find something that will stay with them, or has stayed with them, all of their lives.

CAROL ANN DUFFY

Morning Song

Love set you going like a fat gold watch.
The midwife slapped your footsoles, and your bald cry
Took its place among the elements.

Our voices echo, magnifying your arrival. New statue.
In a draughty museum, your nakedness
Shadows our safety. We stand round blankly as walls.

I'm no more your mother
Than the cloud that distills a mirror to reflect its own slow
Effacement at the wind's hand.

All night your moth-breath
Flickers among the flat pink roses. I wake to listen:
A far sea moves in my ear.

One cry, and I stumble from bed, cow-heavy and floral
In my Victorian nightgown.
Your mouth opens clean as a cat's. The window square

Whitens and swallows its dull stars. And now you try
Your handful of notes;
The clear vowels rise like balloons.

Sylvia Plath

New Child

Wait a while, small voyager
  On the shore, with seapinks and shells.

The boat
  Will take a few summers to build
That you must make your voyage in.

You will learn the names.
That golden light is 'sun' — 'moon'
  The silver light
That grows and dwindles.

And the beautiful small splinters
  That wet the stones, 'rain'.

There is a voyage to make,
  A chart to read,
But not yet, not yet.
  'Daisies' spill from your fingers.
  The night daisies are 'stars'.

The keel is laid, the strakes
  Will be set, in time.
A tree is growing
  That will be a tall mast.

All about you, meantime
The music of humanity,
  The dance of creation
Scored on the chart of the voyage.

The stories, legends, poems
Will be woven to make your sail.

You may hear the beautiful tale of Magnus
  Who took salt on his lip.
Your good angel
  Will be with you on that shore.

Soon, the voyage of EMMA
  To Tir-Nan-Og and beyond.

Star of the Sea, shine on her voyage.

George Mackay Brown

maggie and milly and molly and may

maggie and milly and molly and may
went down to the beach (to play one day)

and maggie discovered a shell that sang
so sweetly she couldn't remember her troubles, and

milly befriended a stranded star
whose rays five languid fingers were;

and molly was chased by a horrible thing
which raced sideways while blowing bubbles: and

may came home with a smooth round stone
as small as a world and as large as alone.

for whatever we lose (like a you or a me)
it's always ourselves we find in the sea

E. E. Cummings

Annabel Lee

It was many and many a year ago,
In a kingdom by the sea,
That a maiden there lived whom you may know
By the name of ANNABEL LEE.
And this maiden she lived with no other thought
Than to love and be loved by me.

I was a child and she was a child
In this kingdom by the sea:
But we loved with a love that was more than love
I and my ANNABEL LEE,
With a love that the wingèd seraphs of heaven
Coveted her and me.

And this was the reason that, long ago,
In this kingdom by the sea,
A wind blew out of a cloud, chilling
My beautiful ANNABEL LEE,
So that her high-born kinsman came
And bore her away from me,
To shut her up in a sepulchre
In this kingdom by the sea.

The angels, not half so happy in heaven,
Went envying her and me —
Yes! That was the reason (as all men know,
In this kingdom by the sea)
That the wind came out of the cloud one night,
Chilling and killing my ANNABEL LEE.

But our love it was stronger by far than the love
Of those who were older than we —
Of many far wiser than we —
And neither the angels in heaven above,
Nor the demons down under the sea,
Can ever dissever my soul from the soul
Of the beautiful ANNABEL LEE:

For the moon never beams without bringing me dreams
Of the beautiful ANNABEL LEE;
And the stars never rise, but I feel the bright eyes
Of the beautiful ANNABEL LEE;
And so, all the night-tide, I lie down by the side
Of my darling — my darling — my life and my bride.
In the sepulchre there by the sea,
In her tomb by the sounding sea.

Edgar Allan Poe

The Wild Trees

O the wild trees of my home,
forests of blue dividing the pink moon,
the iron blue of those ancient branches
with their berries of vermilion stars.

In that place of steep meadows
the stacked sheaves are roasting,
and the sun-torn tulips
are tinders of scented ashes.

But here I have lost
the dialect of your hills,
my tongue has gone blind
far from their limestone roots.

Through trunks of black elder
runs a fox like a lantern,
and the hot grasses sing
with the slumber of larks.

But here there are thickets
of many different gestures,
torn branches of brick and steel
frozen against the sky.

O the wild trees of home
with their sounding dresses,
locks powdered with butterflies
and cheeks of blue moss.

I want to see you rise
from my brain's dry river,
I want your lips of wet roses
laid over my eyes.

O fountains of earth and rock,
gardens perfumed with cucumber,
home of secret valleys
where the wild trees grow.

Let me return at last
to your fertile wilderness,
to sleep with the coiled fernleaves
in your heart's live stone.

Laurie Lee

The Jabberwocky

'Twas brillig, and the slithy toves
Did gyre and gimble in the wabe;
All mimsy were the borogoves,
And the mome raths outgrabe.

'Beware the Jabberwock, my son!
The jaws that bite, the claws that catch!
Beware the jubjub bird, and shun
The frumious bandersnatch!'

He took his vorpal sword in hand:
Long time the manxome foe he sought —
So rested he by the Tumtum tree
And stood awhile in thought.

And as in uffish thought he stood,
The Jabberwock, with eyes of flame,
Came whiffling through the tulgey wood,
And burbled as it came!

The pirate gaped at Belinda's dragon,
And gulped some grog from his pocket flagon,
He fired two bullets but they didn't hit,
And Custard gobbled him, every bit.

Belinda embraced him, Mustard licked him,
No one mourned for his pirate victim.
Ink and Blink in glee did gyrate
Around the dragon that ate the pyrate.

Belinda still lives in her little white house,
With her little black kitten and her little gray mouse,
And her little yellow dog and her little red wagon,
And her realio, trulio, little pet dragon.

Belinda is as brave as a barrel full of bears,
And Ink and Blink chase lions down the stairs,
Mustard is as brave as a tiger in a rage,
But Custard keeps crying for a nice safe cage.

Ogden Nash

The Birds

Do you ask what the birds say?
　　The sparrow, the dove,
The linnet and thrush say:
　　I love and I love.

In the Winter they're silent,
　　The wind is so strong;
What it says I don't know
　　But it sings a loud song.

But green leaves and blossoms,
　　And sunny, warm weather,
And singing, and loving,
　　All come back together.

But the lark is so brimful
　　Of gladness and love,
The green fields below him,
　　The blue sky above.

That he sings and he sings
　　And forever sings he:
I love my love
And my love loves me.

Samuel Taylor Coleridge

The Donkey

When fishes flew and forests walked
    And figs grew upon thorn,
Some moment when the moon was blood
    Then surely I was born.

With monstrous head and sickening cry
    And ears like errant wings,
The devil's walking parody
    On all four-footed things.

The tattered outlaw of the earth,
    Of ancient crooked will;
Starve, scourge, deride me: I am dumb,
    I keep my secret still.

Fools! For I also had my hour,
    One far fierce hour and sweet:
There was a shout about my ears,
    And palms before my feet.

G. K. Chesterton

Lobster Quadrille

'Will you walk a little faster?' said a whiting to a snail.

'There's a porpoise close behind us, and he's treading on my tail.

See how eagerly the lobsters and the turtles all advance!

They are waiting on the shingle — will you come and join the dance?

Will you, won't you, will you, won't you, will you join the dance?

Will you, won't you, will you, won't you, won't you join the dance?'

'You can really have no notion how delightful it will be,

When they take us up and throw us, with the lobsters, out to sea!'

But the snail replied 'Too far, too far!' and gave a look askance —

Said he thanked the whiting kindly, but he would not join the dance.

Would not, could not, would not, could not, would not join the dance.

Would not, could not, would not, could not, could not join the dance.

'What matters it how far we go?' his scaly friend replied.

'There is another shore, you know, upon the other side.

The further off from England the nearer is to France —

Then turn not pale, beloved snail, but come and join the dance.

   Will you, won't you, will you, won't you, will you join the dance?

   Will you, won't you, will you, won't you, won't you join the dance?'

Lewis Carroll

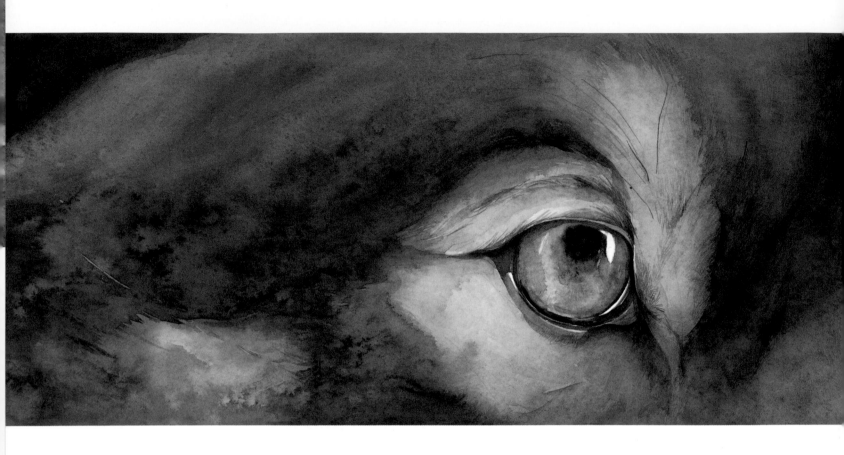

Amulet

Inside the Wolf's fang, the mountain of heather.

Inside the mountain of heather, the Wolf's fur.

Inside the Wolf's fur, the ragged forest.

Inside the ragged forest, the Wolf's foot.

Inside the Wolf's foot, the stony horizon.

Inside the stony horizon, the Wolf's tongue.

Inside the Wolf's tongue, the Doe's tears.

Inside the Doe's tears, the frozen swamp.

Inside the frozen swamp, the Wolf's blood.

Inside the Wolf's blood, the snow wind.

Inside the snow wind, the Wolf's eye.

Inside the Wolf's eye, the North Star.

Inside the North Star, the Wolf's fang.

Ted Hughes

The Tyger

Tyger! Tyger! burning bright
In the forests of the night,
What immortal hand or eye
Could frame thy fearful symmetry?

In what distant deeps or skies
Burnt the fire of thine eyes?
On what wings dare he aspire?
What the hand, dare seize the fire?

And what shoulder, and what art,
Could twist the sinews of thy heart?
And when thy heart began to beat,
What dread hand? and what dread feet?

What the hammer? what the chain?
In what furnace was thy brain?
What the anvil? what dread grasp
Dare its deadly terrors clasp?

When the stars threw down their spears
And watered Heaven with their tears,
Did he smile his work to see?
Did he who made the Lamb make thee?

Tyger! Tyger! burning bright
In the forests of the night,
What immortal hand or eye
Dare frame thy fearful symmetry?

William Blake

Daffodils

I wandered lonely as a cloud
That floats on high o'er vales and hills,
When all at once I saw a crowd,
A host, of golden daffodils.
Beside the lake, beneath the trees,
Fluttering and dancing in the breeze.

Continuous as the stars that shine
And twinkle on the milky way,
They stretched in never-ending line
Along the margin of a bay:
Ten thousand saw I at a glance
Tossing their heads in sprightly dance.

The waves beside them danced, but they
Out-did the sparkling waves in glee:
A poet could not but be gay
In such a jocund company!
I gazed — and gazed — but little thought
What wealth the show to me had brought:

For oft, when on my couch I lie
In vacant or in pensive mood,
They flash upon that inward eye
Which is the bliss of solitude;
And then my heart with pleasure fills,
And dances with the daffodils.

William Wordsworth

from *Song of Myself*

I celebrate myself, and sing myself,
And what I assume you shall assume,
For every atom belonging to me as good belongs to you.

I loafe and invite my soul,
I lean and loafe at my ease observing a spear of summer grass.

My tongue, every atom of my blood, form'd from this soil, this air,
Born here of parents born here from parents the same, and their parents the same,
I, now thirty-seven years old in perfect health begin,
Hoping to cease not till death.
Creeds and schools in abeyance,
Retiring back a while sufficed at what they are, but never forgotten,
I harbor for good or bad, I permit to speak at every hazard,
Nature without check with original energy.

Walt Whitman

Fern Hill

Now as I was young and easy under the apple boughs
About the lilting house and happy as the grass was green,
    The night above the dingle starry,
      Time let me hail and climb
    Golden in the heydays of his eyes,
And honoured among wagons I was prince of the apple towns
And once below a time I lordly had the trees and leaves
      Trail with daisies and barley
    Down the rivers of the windfall light.

And as I was green and carefree, famous among the barns
About the happy yard and singing as the farm was home,
    In the sun that is young once only,
      Time let me play and be
    Golden in the mercy of his means,
And green and golden I was huntsman and herdsman, the calves
Sang to my horn, the foxes on the hills barked clear and cold,
      And the sabbath rang slowly
    In the pebbles of the holy streams.

Until I Saw the Sea

Until I saw the sea

I did not know

that wind

could wrinkle water so.

I never knew

that sun

could splinter a whole sea of blue.

Nor

did I know before

a sea breathes in and out

upon a shore.

Lilian Moore

The Night Mail

This is the night mail crossing the border,
Bringing the cheque and the postal order,
Letters for the rich, letters for the poor,
The shop at the corner and the girl next door,
Pulling up Beattock, a steady climb —
The gradient's against her, but she's on time.

Past cotton grass and moorland boulder,
Shovelling white steam over her shoulder,
Snorting noisily as she passes
Silent miles of wind-bent grasses;
Birds turn their heads as she approaches,
Stare from the bushes at her blank-faced coaches;
Sheepdogs cannot turn her course,
They slumber on with paws across;
In the farm she passes no one wakes
But a jug in the bedroom gently shakes.

Dawn freshens, the climb is done.
Down towards Glasgow she descends
Towards the steam tugs yelping down the glade of cranes
Towards the fields of apparatus, the furnaces
Set on the dark plain like gigantic chessmen.
All Scotland waits for her;
In the dark glens, beside the pale-green sea lochs,
Men long for news.

Letters of thanks, letters from banks,

Letters of joy from the girl and boy,

Receipted bills and invitations

To inspect new stock or visit relations,

And applications for situations,

And timid lovers' declarations,

And gossip, gossip from all the nations,

News circumstantial, news financial,

Letters with holiday snaps to enlarge in,

Letters with faces scrawled in the margin.

Letters from uncles, cousins and aunts,

Letters to Scotland from the South of France,

Letters of condolence to Highlands and Lowlands,

Notes from overseas to Hebrides;

Written on paper of every hue,

The pink, the violet, the white and the blue,

The chatty, the catty, the boring, adoring,

The cold and official and the heart's outpouring.

Clever, stupid, short and long,

The typed and printed and the spelt all wrong.

Thousands are still asleep

Dreaming of terrifying monsters

Or a friendly tea beside the band at Cranston's or Crawford's;

Asleep in working Glasgow, asleep in well-set Edinburgh,

Asleep in granite Aberdeen.

They continue their dreams

But shall wake soon and long for letters.

And none will hear the postman's knock

Without a quickening of the heart,

For who can bear to feel himself forgotten?

W. H. Auden

83

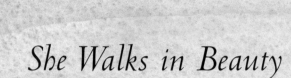

She Walks in Beauty

She walks in beauty, like the night
   Of cloudless chimes and starry skies;
And all that's best of dark and bright
   Meet in her aspect and her eyes:
Thus mellow'd to that tender light
   Which heaven to gaudy day denies.

One shade the more, one ray the less,
   Had half impair'd the nameless grace
Which waves in every raven tress,
   Or softly lightens o'er her face;
Where thoughts serenely sweet express
   How pure, how dear their dwelling place.

And on that cheek, and o'er that brow,
   So soft, so calm, yet eloquent,
The smiles that win, the tints that glow,
   But tell of days in goodness spent,
A mind at peace with all below,
   A heart whose love is innocent!

George Gordon, Lord Byron

He Wishes for the Cloths
of Heaven

Had I the heavens' embroidered cloths,

Enwrought with golden and silver light,

The blue and the dim and the dark cloths

Of night and light and the half-light,

I would spread the cloths under your feet:

But I, being poor, have only my dreams;

I have spread my dreams under your feet;

Tread softly because you tread on my dreams.

W. B. Yeats

How Do I Love Thee?

How do I love thee? Let me count the ways.

I love thee to the depth and breadth and height

My soul can reach, when feeling out of sight

For the ends of Being and ideal Grace.

I love thee to the level of everyday's

Most quiet need, by sun and candle-light.

I love thee freely, as men strive for Right;

I love thee purely, as they turn from Praise.

I love thee with the passion put to use

In my old griefs, and with my childhood's faith.

I love thee with a love I seemed to lose

With my lost saints, — I love thee with the breath,

Smiles, tears, of all my life! — and, if God choose,

I shall but love thee better after death.

Elizabeth Barrett Browning

Sonnet 18

Shall I compare thee to a summer's day?

Thou art more lovely and more temperate:

Rough winds do shake the darling buds of May,

And summer's lease hath all too short a date;

Sometimes too hot the eye of heaven shines,

And often is his gold complexion dimmed;

And every fair from fair sometime declines,

By chance or nature's changing course untrimmed:

But thy eternal summer shall not fade,

Nor lose possession of that fair thou ow'st;

Nor shall death brag thou wander'st in his shade,

When in eternal lines to time thou grow'st:

    So long as men can breathe, or eyes can see,

    So long lives this, and this gives life to thee.

William Shakespeare

Break of Day in the Trenches

The darkness crumbles away.

It is the same old druid Time as ever,

Only a live thing leaps my hand,

A queer sardonic rat,

As I pull the parapet's poppy

To stick behind my ear.

Droll rat, they would shoot you if they knew

Your cosmopolitan sympathies.

Now you have touched this English hand

You will do the same to a German

Soon, no doubt, if it be your pleasure

To cross the sleeping green between.

It seems you inwardly grin as you pass

Strong eyes, fine limbs, haughty athletes,

Less chanced than you for life,

Bonds to the whims of murder,

Sprawled in the bowels of the earth,

The torn fields of France.

What do you see in our eyes

At the shrieking iron and flame

Hurled through still heavens?

What quaver — what heart aghast?

Poppies whose roots are in man's veins

Drop, and are ever dropping;

But mine in my ear is safe —

Just a little white with the dust.

Isaac Rosenberg

The General

'Good-morning, good-morning!' the General said
When we met him last week on our way to the line.
Now the soldiers he smiled at are most of 'em dead,
And we're cursing his staff for incompetent swine.
'He's a cheery old card,' grunted Harry to Jack
As they slogged up to Arras with rifle and pack.

. . . .

But he did for them both by his plan of attack.

Siegfried Sassoon

High Flight

Oh! I have slipped the surly bonds of Earth

And danced the skies on laughter-silvered wings;

Sunward I've climbed, and joined the tumbling

     mirth

Of sun-split clouds — and done a hundred things

You have not dreamed of — wheeled and soared and

      swung

High in sunlit silence. Hov'ring there,

I've chased the shouting wind along, and flung

My eager craft through footless halls of air…

Up, up the long, delirious, burning blue

I've topped the wind-swept heights with easy grace

Where never lark, or even eagle flew —

And, while with silent, lifting mind I've trod

The high untrespassed sanctity of space,

Put out my hand, and touched the face of God.

John Gillespie Magee, Jr.

So We'll Go No More
A-Roving

So we'll go no more a-roving
So late into the night,
Though the heart be still as loving,
And the moon be still as bright.

For the sword outwears its sheath,
And the soul wears out the breast,
And the heart must pause to breathe,
And love itself have rest.

Though the night was made for loving,
And the day returns too soon,
Yet we'll go no more a-roving
By the light of the moon.

George Gordon, Lord Byron

Jenny Kissed Me

Jenny kiss'd me when we met,
Jumping from the chair she sat in;
Time, you thief, who love to get
Sweets into your list, put that in!
Say I'm weary, say I'm sad,
Say that health and wealth have miss'd me,
Say I'm growing old, but add,
Jenny kiss'd me.

Leigh Hunt

Music

Let me go where'er I will

I hear a sky-born music still:

It sounds from all things old,

It sounds from all things young;

From all that's fair, from all that's foul,

Peals out a cheerful song.

It is not only in the bird,

Not only where the rainbow glows,

Nor in the song of woman heard,

But in the darkest, meanest things

There always, always, something sings.

'Tis not in the high stars alone,

Nor in the cups of budding flowers,

Nor in the redbreast's mellow tone,

Nor in the bow that smiles in showers,

But in the mud and scum and things

There always, always, something sings.

Ralph Waldo Emerson

My Heart Leaps Up

My heart leaps up when I behold
A rainbow in the sky:
So was it when my life began;
So is it now I am a man;
So be it when I shall grow old,
Or let me die!
The Child is father of the Man,
And I could wish my days to be
Bound each to each by natural piety.

William Wordsworth

The Road Not Taken

Two roads diverged in a yellow wood,
And sorry I could not travel both
And be one traveller, long I stood
And looked down one as far as I could
To where it bent in the undergrowth;

Then took the other, as just as fair,
And having perhaps the better claim,
Because it was grassy and wanted wear;
Though as for that the passing there
Had worn them really about the same.

And both that morning equally lay
In leaves no step had trodden black.
Oh, I kept the first for another day!
Yet knowing how way leads on to way,
I doubted if I should ever come back.

I shall be telling this with a sigh
Somewhere ages and ages hence:
Two roads diverged in a wood, and I —
I took the one less travelled by,
And that has made all the difference.

Robert Frost

from **The Garden**

What wond'rous Life in this I lead!
Ripe Apples drop about my head;
The Luscious Clusters of the Vine
Upon my Mouth do crush their Wine;
The Nectaren, and curious Peach,
Into my hands themselves do reach;
Stumbling on melons, as I pass,
Insnar'd with Flow'rs, I fall on grass.

Mean while the Mind, from pleasure less,
Withdraws into its happiness:
The Mind, that Ocean where each kind
Does streight its own resemblance find;
Yet it creates, transcending these,
Far other Worlds, and other Seas,
Annihilating all that's made
To a green Thought in a green shade.

Andrew Marvell

Acknowledgements

'maggie and milly and molly and may'. Copyright © 1956, 1984, 1991 by the Trustees for the E. E. Cummings Trust, from *Complete Poems: 1904 – 1962* by E. E. Cummings, edited by George J. Firmage. Used by permission of Liveright Publishing Corporation.

'The Beautiful' by W. H. Davies reprinted by permission of Mrs. H. M. Davies Will Trust, Dee & Griffin.

'Tartary' by Walter de la Mare reprinted by permission of The Literary Trustees of Walter de la Mare and the Society of Authors as their representative.

Samuel French Ltd for 'Moonlit Apples' by John Drinkwater.

'Cats' by Eleanor Farjeon from *Blackbird Has Spoken* published by Macmillan. Reprinted by permission of David Higham Associates.

'The Wild Trees' by Laurie Lee. Reprinted by permission of PDF on behalf of The Estate of Laurie Lee © 1960.

'Cargoes' by John Masefield reprinted by permission of The Society of Authors as the Literary Representative of the Estate of John Masefield.

'The Highwayman' by Alfred Noyes reprinted by permission of The Society of Authors as the Literary Representative of the Estate of Alfred Noyes.

'Spell of Creation' by Kathleen Raine reprinted by permission of Brian Keeble, Literary Executor of the Estate of Kathleen Raine.

'The Paint Box' by E V Rieu reprinted by permission of the Authors Licensing & Collecting Society Ltd on behalf of the estate of the late E V Rieu.

'Oliphaunt' by J. R. R. Tolkien reprinted by permission of HarperCollins Publishers Ltd. © 1962, 1990 by J. R. R. Tolkien.

'Dorothy Dances' by Louis Untermeyer. Permission is granted by arrangement with the Estate of Louise Untermeyer, Norma Anchin Untermeyer c/o Professional Publishing Services. The reprint is granted with the expressed permission by Laurence S. Untermeyer.

'This is Just to Say' by William Carlos Williams from *Collected Poems: 1909-1939, Volume I*, copyright © 1938 published by Carcanet Press Limited. Reprinted by permission of Carcanet Press Limited.

The publishers have made every effort to contact holders of copyright material. If you have not received our correspondence, please contact us for inclusion in future editions.

Barefoot Books
Celebrating Art and Story

At Barefoot Books, we celebrate art and story that opens
the hearts and minds of children from all walks of life, inspiring
them to read deeper, search further, and explore their own creative gifts.
Taking our inspiration from many different cultures, we focus on themes that
encourage independence of spirit, enthusiasm for learning, and sharing of
the world's diversity. Interactive, playful and beautiful, our products
combine the best of the present with the best of the past to
educate our children as the caretakers of tomorrow.

www.barefootbooks.com

Dreams

Hold fast to dreams
For if dreams die
Life is a broken-winged bird
That cannot fly.